ROLE CARDS
White House Staff

August Gennerich 1887-1936

Gus Gennerich was a NY City police officer when he first started to work for Franklin D. Roosevelt. In 1929, he was assigned to protect Governor Roosevelt whenever he was in the city. Shortly after, he was assigned to protect the governor in Albany, NY. Gus was then sent to Washington, D. C. in 1933 to work for the Secret Service, assigned to the White House. He became FDR's bodyguard and personal aide. He and his successor, Agent Thomas Qualters, were responsible for protection and any physical assistance that the president needed. Due to the paralyzing effect of polio on the president, Gennerich and Qualters were required to assist FDR with entering and exiting autos and buildings, in order to minimize the president's disability while he was in the public eye. This physical closeness also led to a personal closeness with FDR.

Gus was traveling with the president in Argentina in 1936. While there, he died suddenly of a heart attack on December 1. FDR canceled all possible engagements for the day and arranged a funeral service at the embassy for the next day. August Gennerich's body was taken back to Washington, D. C. on the cruiser, U.S.S. *Indianapolis.*

White House Staff

Frances Perkins 1882 -1965

Frances Perkins was the first woman member of any presidential cabinet. Perkins was Secretary of Labor from 1933 to 1945. She and Secretary of the Interior, Harold Ickes, were the only cabinet members to remain in FDR's cabinet for all 4 of his terms.

In her early career, Frances Perkins was active in the fight for women's suffrage and other social issues. In 1911, Perkins was involved with the Investigating Commission of NY, examining the conditions and causes of the Triangle shirtwaist factory fire in NY City. This was a defining moment in her career. When Alfred E. Smith was elected governor of NY in 1918, he appointed her to the New York State Industrial Board. This was a first for a woman.

In 1928, Governor Roosevelt promoted Frances Perkins to the post of industrial commissioner. In 1933, President Roosevelt asked her to serve as his secretary of labor. Perkins saw her authority as secretary of labor more in terms of promoting the general welfare of American workers than encouraging the growth of the decade's labor movement. Frances Perkins was instrumental in drafting some of the New Deal's most important labor legislation, one of which was the 1935 Social Security Act. After her government service, Perkins worked as a labor professor at Cornell University until her death. Frances Perkins died in NY in 1965.

James A. Farley 1888 -1976

James Farley's early life was one of hard work. His father died when he was 11 years old. He and his 4 brothers worked at odd jobs in the brickyards to help his mother and the family. Farley attended public schools, finished high school, and went on to complete business school in bookkeeping. In 1911, he became town clerk of Grassy Point, NY. During the next 17 years he held various state and party offices and became secretary of the Democratic State Committee in 1928.

FDR asked Farley to run his 1928 campaign for New York governor. Farley grew close to both Roosevelt's. Working closely with ER and the Democratic Party Women's Division, Farley helped FDR to win the NY governorship in 1928 and in 1930; and to secure his nomination and election to the presidency in 1932. FDR appointed Farley postmaster general and Democratic party chairman in 1933, and he became one of FDR's closest political advisors.

Farley's close relationship with FDR ended in 1940 because Farley opposed FDR's pursuit of a third term, and because FDR believed that Farley had presidential ambitions of his own. In 1940, Jim Farley resigned his positions to pursue his own unsuccessful bid for the presidency. He remained active in party politics for the rest of his life. James A. Farley died in NY in 1976.

William D. Leahy 1875 - 1959

William Leahy was Admiral of the fleet, chief of staff to the commander in chief, and principal military assistant to President Roosevelt during most of World War II.
Admiral Leahy, who served as counsel between the president and the joint chiefs of staff, played a vital role in the coordination of political purpose and military strategy during wartime. His acquaintance with Franklin Roosevelt dated to 1913, when Roosevelt was Assistant Secretary of the Navy and Leahy was serving in a key position in the Navy Dept.

He capped his career as chief of naval operations in 1937-39, laying the groundwork for the tremendous expansion of the Navy in World War II. On his mandatory retirement in 1939, President Roosevelt awarded Admiral Leahy the Distinguished Service Medal.

In June of 1942, FDR asked Leahy to return to government service as his chief of staff. Of equal value was his close and trusting relationship with President Roosevelt. He was at FDR's side during all of his wartime travels. After FDR's death in 1945, Leahy served President Truman until his final retirement in 1949. Admiral William D. Leahy died in Maryland in 1959.

Ross McIntire 1889 - 1959

Vice Admiral Ross T. McIntire was recommended as a physician to FDR by Admiral Cary Grayson, who had been President Woodrow Wilson's physician. He became the personal physician of President Roosevelt in 1935, and held that position until FDR's death in 1945. This required that he travel with the president.

In 1938, FDR also appointed McIntire surgeon general of the navy and chief of the bureau of medicine and surgery. He also traveled with the president as his official personal physician.

After leaving the navy in 1947, he organized the American Red Cross blood programs. McIntire went on to other administrative work in the medical field. He spent his last years as executive director of the International College of Surgeons. Vice Admiral Ross T. McIntire died in Illinois in 1959.

William D. Hassett 1880 - 1965

William "Bill" Hassett was a correspondence secretary and sometime press secretary to FDR from 1935 to 1945. He began his career as a newspaper reporter, working for several papers over the years. He joined the White House staff in 1935 as an assistant to Press Secretary Steven Early. FDR swore him in as secretary in 1944.

Hassett and Roosevelt were friends from the time of FDR's years as assistant secretary of the Navy. Bill Hassett traveled with FDR which included many trips to Hyde Park. He kept a detailed diary of his trips and then wrote about them in his book, *Off the Record with F. D. R., 1942 -1945.*

Hassett was with FDR in Warm Springs, GA on the day of his death, April 12, 1945. It was he who called the reporters into the Little White House there to inform them of the president's death. He remained as a secretary under President Harry Truman and retired in 1952. William D. Hassett died in Vermont in 1965.

Edwin M. Watson 1883 - 1945

Major General Edwin M. Watson ("Pa") was military aide to President Roosevelt throughout his presidency. In 1939, he also became secretary to the president.

Watson's great personal charm and story-telling ability endeared him to FDR. He then remained in his position rather that being rotated out, as was the custom for military aides. From 1939 on, Watson served in his unusual dual role. Without the title, Pa effectively served as appointments secretary and was a friendly guardian of the president's time.

As FDR's presidency continued during WW II, more and more of his inner circle at the White House died. Major General Edwin Martin Watson died from a stroke aboard the cruiser *Quincy,* while returning from the Yalta Conference in 1945. This saddened FDR immensely and added to his growing loss of friends.

Marvin H. McIntyre 1878 - 1943

Marvin McIntyre was a key insider, one of the so-called "Cufflinks Gang" who first worked for FDR in his 1920 vice-presidential campaign. They formed the core of FDR's White House staff. "Mac" met Assistant Secretary of the Navy FDR when he took over the Navy Department's press relations in 1917.

McIntyre served as assistant secretary to FDR from 1933 until 1937. Then he became secretary to the president until his own death in 1943. His service on the staff of the *Army and Navy Journal* from 1920 to1932 gave him easy access to Washington, D. C. activities, and military circles, which served the White House well.

Mac was in charge of political appointments for FDR, until ill health reduced his ability to be active in that role. However, he continued to handle confidential matters for the president until his death. Marvin Hunter McIntyre died **in Washington, D. C. in 1943.**

White House Staff

Steven T. Early 1889 - 1951

Steve Early was the first White House Press Secretary in history. He served under Franklin D. Roosevelt from 1933 to 1945, and under President Harry S. Truman in 1950. From 1913 to 1917, when Early was the Associated Press correspondent covering the Navy Department, he became acquainted with Assistant Secretary of the Navy, Franklin Delano Roosevelt.

After the election of 1932, FDR asked him to serve as one of the White House Secretaries, and be responsible for press relations. Early held that post throughout the Roosevelt years, leaving government service June 1, 1945.

In the Truman administration, he served as under secretary and later deputy secretary of defense from April 1949 to June 1950. In December 1950 Early was briefly Press Secretary to President Truman, filling in after the sudden death of Charles G. Ross. Stephen Tyree Early died in Washington, D. C. in 1951.

White House Staff

Marguerite LeHand 1898 - 1944

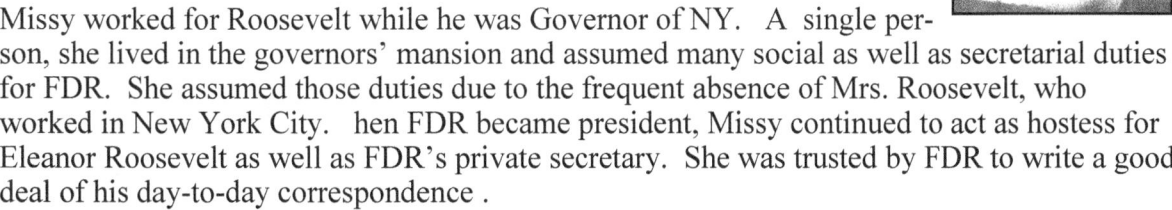

Named "Missy" by the Roosevelt children, Marguerite LeHand was FDR's private secretary from 1920 until 1941. She met FDR while working for the Democratic National Headquarters. After the Democratic defeat of 1920 (including FDR's own), FDR hired her.

Missy worked for Roosevelt while he was Governor of NY. A single person, she lived in the governors' mansion and assumed many social as well as secretarial duties for FDR. She assumed those duties due to the frequent absence of Mrs. Roosevelt, who worked in New York City. hen FDR became president, Missy continued to act as hostess for Eleanor Roosevelt as well as FDR's private secretary. She was trusted by FDR to write a good deal of his day-to-day correspondence .

Missy managed the president's accounts for him, actually paying his bills by check. Her opinion was sought and valued by other staff members. Missy often traveled to Hyde Park with the Roosevelts. Her devotion to work caused her health problems. In 1941 Missy suffered a severe stroke. She never fully recovered. Marguerite LeHand died in Massachusetts in 1944.

Malvina Thompson 1893 - 1953

Malvina Thompson was Eleanor Roosevelt's trusted assistant, secretary, traveling companion, gatekeeper, and dear friend. She was nicknamed "Tommy" by Anna Roosevelt.

Thompson joined the staff of the New York State Democratic Committee, working part-time. She helped ER generate a solid women's turnout for Al Smith's 1928 presidential campaign. Utterly devoted to ER, Thompson organized her life around her boss.

By the time they moved to the White House, the two women had built an amazing work partnership and friendship. Tommy had no time for a personal life; she was divorced as a result of her dedication to her work for ER. When ER had the Val-Kill furniture factory converted into living quarters, she had a two bedroom apartment designed there for Thompson's use.

With her no-nonsense approach to life and work, Tommy became an advisor and sounding board for ER and her family. Tommy died in NY on April 12, 1953, FDR's death date.

Grace Tully 1900 - 1984

Grace Tully called herself, "number two girl" while she worked in FDR's office. Missy LeHand was the president's private secretary and Grace assisted Missy with shorthand and typing assignments.

Grace first worked for Eleanor Roosevelt through the Democratic National Committee during the presidential election of 1928, then worked for Governor Roosevelt. After Missy became ill in 1941, "Tully" or "child" as FDR liked to call her, became private secretary to FDR in Missy's place.

Like others of the staff, Tully would dine with the family and travel to Hyde Park and other places with them. Tully was present at Warm Springs, GA where FDR died on April 12, 1945. After the president's death, Grace lived in Washington, D. C., and wrote a book about her experiences. She became secretary for both Senator Lyndon Johnson and Senator Mike Mansfield. Grace Tully died in Washington, D. C. in 1984.

Robert McGaughey

Robert McGaughey came from Ireland in April of 1922. He was interviewed by Sara Delano Roosevelt and within a month he found himself in Hyde Park, where he remained for the rest of his life. He married one of the house maids, Isabel MacArthur, and they lived together with their 2 boys in an apartment over the stable at Springwood. Robert was hired as the "houseman", a term for a person who did many household chores as needed.

Later, McGuaghey became Sara Roosevelt's butler. A butler is head of household staff and has more responsibilities as well as work. Sara Roosevelt often had long-term servants work in other capacities and to "fill-in" where needed at Springwood. McGuaghey would open the house for the Roosevelts in the spring for their return from NY City. This required a lot of work including supervision of and assisting with the housecleaning; kitchen and meal preparations; and the general orderliness of the home.

After polio left FDR disabled, he recovered at Springwood. Robert was assigned to assist in FDR's care in the first year of recovery. This meant lifting and carrying him in and out of cars and other places, fireman style, with the help of the chauffeur. After FDR's death in 1945, Robert and Isabel McGaughey worked for the National Park Service at Springwood.

William Plog 1869 -1952

William Plog was hired as a gardener by Mr. and Mrs. James Roosevelt (FDR's parents) in 1897. William and his wife, Josephine, were newlyweds when they arrived. The Plogs lived in a cottage on the Springwood estate. Sara Roosevelt often had long-term servants work in other capacities and to "fill-in" where needed at Springwood. In later years, Josephine Plog would assist with various household activities for Sara Roosevelt.

As the years went by, Plog became head gardener, then superintendent of the estate. With the promotions came more work and responsibility. Plog supervised the gardeners, the wood-cutters, the ice-harvesting from the pond, looked after the greenhouses, and sent cut roses to Sara Roosevelt at her NY City townhouse. The Plogs were so trusted by the Roosevelts that they were asked to live in Springwood rather than in their own cottage while the family was in NY or traveling.

When FDR died on April 12, 1945, Plog had the sad task of preparing the rose garden for the president's gravesite. This was FDR's own request. When Springwood became the property of the National Park Service, Plog was employed by the government as foreman of buildings and grounds. He died in NY in 1952.

House Staff

Russell Linaka

Russell W. Linaka was a Navy man who took care of three greenhouses and 100 acres of land around the Naval Observatory in Washington, D. C. At the advice of Admiral William D. Leahy, President Roosevelt's chief of staff, FDR quickly persuaded him to retire and take over the neglected tree plantation in Hyde Park.

FDR used his family estate to experiment with forestry and soil conservation practices. Conservation became an interest of FDR's while he was serving as NY state senator, his first public office. The president called on the advice and services of Dr. Nelson C. Brown of the NY State College of Forestry. With Brown's advice and Linaka's supervision, there were immediate results. More than 100,000 trees were in the ground within two years. After the war they planted another 38,000 trees.

Part of FDR's plans for retirement included income from the thousands of Christmas trees which were planted. Mr. Linaka said, "…after they got 2 or 3 feet high, he (FDR) could sit in his car and look at them. Row upon row…He loved to see those straight lines of trees."

After FDR's death in 1945, Russell Linaka continued to manage the estate farm and tree plantations for Mrs. Roosevelt and Elliott Roosevelt.

Friend

Henry Morgenthau, Jr. 1891 -1967

Henry Morgenthau, Jr. and his wife Elinor were close friends and neighbors of the Roosevelts. The 2 men shared a common interest in agricultural improvement and rural political strength.

His friendship with FDR led to a variety of governmental appointments at the state and national levels leading to his position as Secretary of the Treasury from 1934-1945. His work at Treasury created controversy during the Depression as did his plan for dealing with Germany at the end of WWII.

Morgenthau's legacy is greater than wartime financial policy. Morgenthau and his department played a key role in American refugee policy when they helped convince FDR to establish an independent refugee agency outside the State Department known as the War Refugee Board. The War Refugee Board, not the State Department, would assume responsibility for rescuing European Jews and would take the lead in saving as many as 200,000 people during WW II. After leaving the cabinet in 1945, Morgenthau became a philanthropist and a leading financial advisor to the new nation of Israel. He died in New York in 1967.

Henry Noble MacCracken 1870 -1970

In 1915, MacCracken became the fifth president of Vassar College. Mac-Cracken wore many hats during his lifetime: Not only president of Vassar, he was founder of the American Junior Red Cross; head of the NY Temporary Emergency Relief Foundation; and the director of the National Conference of Christians and Jews. He also assisted in founding Sarah Lawrence College.

He met and became friends with the Roosevelts in the 1920's. He and FDR loved early American history and enjoyed collaborating in Dutchess County Historical Society projects. Henry and FDR were connected because Roosevelt was an active and honorary trustee of Vassar College from 1923 until his death in 1945.

Internationalism and pacifism were large themes in Henry's life. MacCracken invited the 2nd World Youth Congress to meet at Vassar College in August, 1938. Its purpose: to exchange youths' ideas in order to unite in action for preventing war. Some politicians accused the group of being communist,. From nearby Hyde Park Eleanor Roosevelt came to address the delegates. She returned later that week as a member of the audience.

MacCracken retired from Vassar College in 1946. Henry N. MacCracken died in New York in 1970.

Thomas G. Corcoran 1900 -1981

A graduate of Harvard Law School with a doctoral degree, Thomas Corcoran worked as a law clerk for Supreme Court Justice Oliver Wendell Holmes, a position obtained through the aid of his law professor, Felix Frankfurter. Frankfurter brought him to FDR's attention in 1933, during work on securities legislation.

He assisted in placing able, young attorneys in civil service jobs for the New Deal agencies during FDR's presidency. His legal and political networking abilities have identified him as one of the first congressional lobbyists.

FDR nicknamed him "Tommy the Cork" because of his lobbying skills. In 1932, he was on the legal staff of the Reconstruction Finance Corporation . While there, he acted unofficially as FDR's adviser, friend, and political ally until 1940. After the president's re-election in 1940 ,"Tommy the Cork" Corcoran was out of government work and in private law practice, while remaining personally close to FDR. It is said that he left government over his objections to FDR's "court packing plan" of 1937. Thomas G. Corcoran died in Washington, D. C. in 1981.

Elizabeth Fisher Read 1872-1943

A scholar and one of Eleanor Roosevelt's earliest female political and feminist mentors, Elizabeth Read was ER's personal attorney and financial advisor during the first part of her public career. Eleanor credited Read and Esther Lape, Read's life partner, with playing an important role in her education as a political activist.

With her legal, political, and social reform activism and abilities, Elizabeth provided important information and insight to Franklin Roosevelt as well.   Read first worked with Eleanor when ER became director of the League of Women Voters national legislation committee in 1920. Impressed with one another's skills, abilities and brains, the women quickly cemented what became both a political partnership and a warm friendship.

Read and Lape visited both Springwood and Val-Kill over the years of friendship with the Roosevelts. Elizabeth Read died in New York in1943.

Esther Lape 1881-1981

Esther Lape was a graduate of Wellesley College. She taught English at several universities and colleges. She was well known as a journalist, researcher, and publicist. Lape was also associated with the Women's Trade Union League and one of the founders of the League of Women Voters. Her life partner was the scholar and lawyer, Elizabeth Read.

Eleanor credited Lape and Read with playing an important role in her education as a political activist. It was through Read that ER met Lape and a professional relationship between Lape, Read, and ER was established in 1920. With her political, public relations, and social reform activism and abilities, Esther provided important information and insight to Franklin Roosevelt as well. Impressed with one another's skills, abilities and brains, the women quickly cemented what became both a political partnership and a warm friendship.

Read and Lape visited both Springwood and Val-Kill over the years of friendship with the Roosevelts. Esther Lape died in New York in 1981.

Elinor F. Morgenthau 1892 -1949

Wife of Henry Morgenthau, Jr., who was Secretary of the Treasury from 1934 to the end of FDR's presidency, Elinor and Henry were Roosevelt friends and neighbors in Dutchess County.

In the 1920s, Elinor Morgenthau was not only a neighbor, but also part of an influential political alliance with Eleanor Roosevelt and her friends in the Democratic Committee in NY state. In 1928 she was a delegate to the Democratic National Convention. By the 1930s, Elinor Morgenthau was a frequent riding and traveling companion of ER's.

Elinor was a Vassar College graduate with an interest in fine arts. She assisted the arts program within the Works Progress Administration (WPA) during the Depression. She also wrote for the National Gallery of Art. ER reflected on their lives: "She was my friend over a great many years. I can look back on many pleasures and good times as well as on fruitful working periods that we both enjoyed". Elinor Morgenthau died in New York in 1949.

Francis Biddle 1886 -1968

Francis Biddle and FDR both graduated Groton School, Harvard College, and worked in the law. Biddle, however, clerked at the Supreme Court and practiced law for years. They both belonged to "old money" families. Biddle was a frequent guest at Springwood.

At first a Republican, in 1932, he switched loyalty to the Democratic Party. Francis strongly supported FDR and the New Deal.

Biddle, a collector of fine art, suggested that the New Deal program, the Works Project Administration, should include jobs for fine artists. The president appointed Francis to several different Justice Department positions, the last being Attorney General. He served in this position throughout most of World War II.

After FDR's death in 1945, President Truman appointed Biddle as a judge at the WW II International Military Tribunal at Nuremberg, Germany. Francis Biddle died in Massachusetts in 1968.

Bernard M. Baruch 1870 -1965

Financier, public official, and philanthropist, Bernard was a friend and adviser to the Roosevelts. He was often a guest at Springwood.

He became a multimillionaire by his mid-thirties through his stock investments. He chose to devote himself to public affairs, usually preferring to act as a personal consultant . He continued to advise every president from Wilson through Kennedy.

He accepted President Franklin Roosevelt's offer to chair a committee on war mobilization legislation in 1934. After World War II, he accepted an appointment from President Harry Truman as ambassador to the United Nations Atomic Energy Commission in 1946. He preferred his near-legendary role as "Mr. Baruch", offering advice to people including presidents. He did this from a park bench near the White House in Washington, D. C. Bernard Mannes Baruch died in New York in 1965.

Daniel Basil O'Connor 1892 -1972

Basil O'Connor graduated Harvard Law School and began to practice law in 1915. He met FDR in the early 1920's in NY and became his legal advisor. In 1924, the two men formed their own law firm which existed until Roosevelt's first inauguration in 1933.

In 1921, FDR became ill with polio, which paralyzed his legs. In 1927, FDR founded the polio treatment center known as the Georgia Warm Springs Foundation with O'Connor as his partner. In 1938, the 2 men joined to form the National Foundation for Infantile Paralysis.

Due to his involvement in medical foundations and their research, Basil's nickname was "Doc". The National Foundation for Infantile Paralysis focused on supporting research for polio prevention and treatment. The foundation became famous because of its fundraising radio campaign "March of Dimes" with its appeal to Americans to donate one dime for the fight against polio. Since 1979, the foundation's name has been March of Dimes. That's why FDR's image is on the dime today. "Doc" and his family often visited Springwood. Basil O'Connor died in Arizona in 1972.

John E. Mack 1874 - 1958

John E. Mack was instrumental in many defining moments of FDR's life, most of them political; he was FDR's friend as well. He was a well-respected lawyer, whose practice was statewide; a district attorney, a politician involved in Dutchess County's Democratic Party; and a NY Supreme Court judge, thanks to his friend Franklin Roosevelt.

Franklin Roosevelt recalled that in August, 1910, on a very hot day…"In front of the courthouse I ran across a group of friends of mine. … as I remember, they took me out to the policemen's picnic in Fairview. (Cont'd …)On that joyous occasion of clams and sauerkraut and real beer - on that great occasion I made my first political speech..."

Mack recalled being impressed by Roosevelt, and suggested to him that he run for state assembly from the Mid-Hudson area. He told Roosevelt he would have a 1 in 5 chance for victory in a race for the State Senate. FDR was elected as state senator in 1910, and re-elected in 1912.In1932, John Mack placed the name of his friend in nomination for the presidency of the United States. "I am very happy that my old friend and neighbor John E. Mack has been good enough to say that he will make the nominating speech in my behalf at the Democratic National Convention." Judge John E. Mack died at Poughkeepsie, NY in 1958.

Louis M. Howe 1871 - 1936

Louis Howe was Franklin and Eleanor Roosevelt's most important political mentor and friend. Louis was a newspaper reporter from Saratoga, NY. Reporting introduced him to his passion: politics. From the minute he met him in 1911, Louis knew that FDR would someday be a president of the U. S., and that he would get FDR there.

When polio paralyzed FDR in 1921, Howe stood by his friend to help restore him to health, to return to politics, and support ER in her efforts. Louis' and Eleanor's efforts, convinced NY Governor Alfred E. Smith that FDR must be his successor as governor. During FDR's 4 years in Albany, Howe worked nonstop to secure the 1932 Democratic presidential nomination for FDR. FDR's victory meant almost as much to Howe as it did to FDR. It was his life's work. His dedication to the Roosevelts overshadowed his own family life with his wife and 2 children.

Louis McHenry Howe died at Washington, D.C. in 1936. ER arranged a state funeral in the White House for her friend, whom she would describe as "one of the seven most important people" in her life.

Helen W. Reynolds 1875 - 1943

FDR's involvement in local history brought him in contact with Helen Wilkinson Reynolds. Besides their common interest in regional history, both were physically handicapped. They were founding members of the Dutchess Co. Historical Society. Reynolds and FDR would spend Sundays picnicking on his estate in what they called ''historical afternoons.''

In 1923, Helen Reynolds and FDR collaborated on a book about the history of Dutch-style homes in the valley. To be sure, their collaboration found Helen Reynolds doing most of the actual work as FDR had perfected the art of delegation well before his White House years.

When FDR was called to the presidency, his connection with Hudson Valley history was through Helen Reynolds. They corresponded frequently and on many visits to Hyde Park, time was found for visits with her. FDR planned for her to become the curator of documents related to local history to be housed at the FDR Library. It was not to be, as Helen died in 1943.

FDR remarked, "She was a good friend and we had worked together so much on things related to Dutchess County that I shall greatly miss her."

Harry L. Hopkins 1890 - 1946

Harry began his career as a social worker in 1912. Until 1931, he held various positions for public health care and child welfare organizations. He cared very deeply for the relief of hunger, poverty, and ill-health among the nation's needy. He often pushed himself to exhaustion at the expense of his own health.

Harry Hopkins was introduced to Governor Roosevelt by Eleanor. The two men soon developed a close working association and friendship. In1931, Governor Franklin D. Roosevelt named Harry Hopkins to be head of the NY State Temporary Relief Agency.

In the spring of 1933, President Roosevelt turned to Hopkins to organize public relief from the Great Depression on a national scale. During the years 1933-38, Harry served administratively for FDR at several of the "Alphabet Agencies". During WW II he became FDR's special assistant for various projects. Due to ill health, Harry Hopkins had to leave FDR's service in March, 1945. The two men never saw each other again. FDR died on April 12, 1945.

President Truman awarded Harry L. Hopkins the Distinguished Service Medal in September, 1945. He died in January, 1946

Nancy Cook 1884 -1962

Nancy Cook is most known for her relationship with Eleanor Roosevelt. In fact, she was a friend to both Roosevelts and she and her life partner, Marion Dickerman spent many years in the company of the entire Roosevelt family. She attended Syracuse University, where she became an activist for women's rights and reform of labor laws. After graduation, she taught.

Her life of activism continued as she and Marion volunteered during WWI in England, and then on to women's Democratic politics in NY state. In 1922, Nancy and ER met at a luncheon for the NY Democratic Women's Division. Nancy and Marion became 2 of ER's early political mentors. Soon Cook and Dickerman became frequent guests of the Roosevelts. By 1925 the three women, built a stone cottage 2 miles east of Springwood on land that FDR provided, named Val-Kill. Cook and Dickerman made Stone Cottage their home.

ER, Nancy, and Marion became partners in Val-Kill Industries, a business created to give jobs to Hyde Park youth. This furniture and pewter factory was built behind the Stone Cottage **at** Val-Kill. Some Val-Kill furniture can be seen on the 2nd floor of Springwood.

In 1947, Nancy and Marion sold their interest in Val-Kill to ER and moved to New Canaan, Connecticut.

Marion Dickerman 1890 -1983

Marion Dickerman is most known for her relationship with Eleanor Roosevelt. In fact, she was a friend to both Roosevelts and she and her life partner, Nancy Cook spent many years in the company of the entire Roosevelt family. She attended Syracuse University, where she became an activist for women's rights and reform of labor laws. After graduation, she taught.

Her life of activism continued as she and Nancy volunteered during WWI in England, and then on to women's Democratic politics in NY state. By summer 1922, Marion joined the faculty of the Todhunter School in NY City. The school became a joint project for Marion and ER in later years. Marion met ER in June 1922 when she accompanied Nancy, then involved in NY Democratic women's politics, to Hyde Park for a weekend visit. Soon Dickerman and Cook became frequent guests of the Roosevelts. By 1925 the three women, built a stone cottage 2 miles east of Springwood on land that FDR provided, named Val-Kill. Cook and Dickerman made Stone Cottage their home.

ER, Nancy, and Marion became partners in Val-Kill Industries, a business created to give jobs to Hyde Park youth. This furniture and pewter factory was built behind the Stone Cottage at Val-Kill. Some Val-Kill furniture can be seen on the 2nd floor of Springwood. In 1947, Marion and Nancy sold their interest in Val-Kill to ER and moved to New Canaan, Connecticut. Marion died in Pennsylvania in 1983.

Winston Churchill 1874 -1965

Winston Churchill was appointed Prime Minister of Great Britain in 1940. The close friendship and excellent working relations that developed between FDR and Churchill were key in the founding of a unified effort to deal with the Axis (enemy) powers in WW II. FDR wanted to support Britain and believed the United States should serve as a "great arsenal of democracy."

In January 1941 Roosevelt proposed a new military aid bill to Congress. This Lend-Lease Act was passed by Congress in March 1941. It went a long way toward solving the concerns of both Great Britain's desperate need for supplies and America's desire to appear neutral. In August 1941, Roosevelt and Churchill met for the first of nine face-to-face conferences during WW II.

From 1941 when they first met, until FDR's death in 1945, Roosevelt and Churchill continued a close personal and professional relationship. Churchill later wrote, "I felt I was in contact with a very great man who was also a warm-hearted friend and the foremost champion of the high causes which we served." Winston Churchill visited Springwood on 5 separate occasions and once after FDR's death. He traveled here with his family on some of those visits. Sir Winston Churchill died in England in 1965.

Mackenzie King 1874 - 1950

Mackenzie King was 10th Prime Minister of Canada from 1921 to 1948. King earned 5 university degrees. He is the second Prime Miister of Canada to earn a doctorate. He taught Economics at Harvard. In his early career, he traveled back and forth to the U. S. working in private industry.

The prime minister was responsible for providing information to FDR which prompted the president to invite King George VI and Queen Elizabeth to visit the U. S. after their visit to Canada in 1939. It was agreed that the American phase of the visit should take place towards the end of the visit to Canada—June 8 - 11, 1939. King was concerned about who should accompany the royals to the U.S. Roosevelt told Mackenzie King that he would accompany the King and Queen to the USA. FDR also wanted him to stay at Hyde Park with them and his family. His title for the trip was Minister in Attendance. The most significant part of the trip for him was the visit to Hyde Park over the weekend of June 10 and 11. Roosevelt, George VI, and Mackenzie King were able to talk about the international situation quite freely. After their return to Canada, George VI asked Mackenzie King for his opinion of the American trip. He replied that he thought "it had surpassed all expectations". Mackenzie King died in Canada in 1950.

Madame Chiang Kai-shek 1897 - 2003

Mayling Soong, who became Madame Chiang Kai-shek, was one of the most influential women of the twentieth century. She and her father were educated in the U. S. She was a graduate of Wellesley College. Mayling met Chiang Kai-shek in 1920. He was eleven years her elder, and a Buddhist. She married him in 1929, after his conversion to Christianity. Madame Chiang was her husband's English translator, secretary, advisor, and an influential propagandist for the Nationalist cause.

In February 1943, Madame Chiang became the first Chinese national, and the second woman, to ever address a joint session of the U.S. House and Senate, making the case for strong U.S. support of China in its war with Japan. During that visit to the U. S., Madame Chiang needed medical treatment in New York City. The Roosevelts offered her the use of Springwood for a recuperation period. She and her staff stayed in Hyde Park for several days. She also spent time in the White House. Chiang Kai-shek declared Taipei, Taiwan to be the temporary capital of China, where he was elected president. Madame Chiang continued to play a prominent international role. President Chiang Kai-shek died in 1975. Following her husband's death, Madame Chiang returned to the U.S. She died in New York in 2003.

Dignitary

Crown Princess Martha 1901 - 1954

Princess Martha of Sweden married   Crown Prince Olav of Norway (later King Olav V) on March 21, 1929, becoming Crown Princess of Norway. In 1939, just before World War II broke out in Europe, she toured the upper midwest of the US with Prince Olav. While in the US, they became friends of Franklin and Eleanor Roosevelt. During WW II their friendship with the Roosevelts benefited both countries. Princess Martha and her husband had three children: Harald, Ragnhild and Astrid.

- When German troops invaded Norway in 1940, they fled to her native Sweden where she was not well received. It was thought that her return would place Sweden's war neutrality at risk.

- After receiving an invitation from President Roosevelt, she and her children left for the United States.

- When first in the U.S., she and the children lived in the White House. Their friendship with the Roosevelts was further developed during those years.

King George VI 1895 –1952

George VI succeeded to the throne unexpectedly after the abdication of his brother, King Edward VIII, in 1936. In 1939, the King and Queen traveled through Canada and then on to the US. George was the 1st king to visit these countries. They were the guests of the Roosevelts that June.

The goal of the tour was mainly political: to build up support for Britain as they confronted the coming of WW II. This was FDR's objective as well; he was faced with national isolationism as a result of WW I. He knew the necessity of being prepared. The King and Queen were enthusiastically and warmly received by the American people. They visited the 1939 World's Fair in NY City, and from there came to Springwood for a relaxing and un-official visit with the Roosevelts.

Eleanor Roosevelt provided them with a glimpse of American life by hosting a picnic at Top Cottage, FDR's retreat. Even though the picnic menu included many regional American foods, the only thing the press chose to report was that the royal couple were served hot dogs to eat! The visit was a success. The newspapers were glowing in their reports of the young royal couple. This enabled FDR to propose legislation in Congress to aid England in WW II, known as the Lend-Lease Act. In September 1939, Germany invaded Poland and England declared war on Germany. The King died in England in 1952.

Queen Elizabeth 1900 –2002

Lady Elizabeth Bowes-Lyon was the Queen Consort of George VI of Great Britain from 1936 until his death in 1952. After her husband's death, she was known as Queen Elizabeth, The Queen Mother, in relation to her daughter, Queen Elizabeth II. As Queen Consort, Elizabeth was famous for her role in providing moral support to the British public during WW II.

In 1939, the King and Queen traveled through Canada and then on to the US. King George was the 1st king to visit these countries. They were the guests of the Roosevelts that June. The goal of the tour was mainly political: to build up support for Britain as they confronted the coming of WW II. They visited the 1939 World's Fair in NY City, and from there came to Springwood for a relaxing and unofficial visit with the Roosevelts.

Eleanor Roosevelt provided them with a glimpse of American life by hosting a picnic at Top Cottage, FDR's retreat. Even though the picnic menu included many regional American foods, the only thing the press chose to report was that the royal couple were served hot dogs to eat! The visit was a success. The newspapers were glowing in their reports of the young royal couple. This enabled FDR to propose legislation in Congress to aid England in WW II, known as the Lend-Lease Act. In September 1939, Germany invaded Poland and England declared war on Germany. The Queen died in England in 2002.

Prince Gustaf Adolf 1882 –1973

The Swedish Crown Prince and Princess were the first royals to visit America during FDR's presidential years. Their visit during July 1938 involved the celebration of 300 years of Swedish life in America. The Prince and Princess were invited to Hyde Park and a dinner was given for them at Springwood.

ER wrote, "The people of Europe were deeply troubled … and were looking for friends in other parts of the world — hence their sudden interest in the US." The policy of Sweden during World War II was to remain neutral. This was not easy to maintain, given the German Nazi presence in Europe. Sweden owed this maintenance of neutrality to its long-held neutral stance in international relations, and a dedicated military build-up.

The German authorities decided to deport the Danish Jewish population to concentration camps. In 1943, Sweden rescued nearly all of Denmark's 8000 Jews. There they were granted asylum. Prince Gustaf Adolf officially negotiated with the Germans during the war. Public opinion believed him to be a Nazi sympathizer — there is no evidence to support that belief. He died in Sweden in 1973.

Princess Louise 1889 –1965

The Swedish Crown Prince and Princess were the first royals to visit America during FDR's presidential years. Their visit during July 1938 involved the celebration of 300 years of Swedish life in America. The Prince and Princess were invited to Hyde Park and a dinner was given for them at Springwood.

ER wrote, "The people of Europe were deeply troubled … and were looking for friends in other parts of the world — hence their sudden interest in the US." During the Finnish Winter War of 1939, when the Russians invaded Finland, Finnish children were sent to Sweden for safety. Princess Louise arranged for a children's home on the grounds of one of the palaces. There she often visited, participating in the children's daily games. After the war, she kept contact with the Finnish children and visited them in Helsinki in their adult life.

When Princess Louise's husband became King Gustaf VI Adolf of Sweden in 1950, she became Queen Louise of Sweden. She died in Sweden in 1965.

Prince Olav 1903 –1991

At the coming of WW II, FDR invited royal families to stay in the U. S. Their lives were at risk due to Nazi occupation of their countries.

ER wrote that "he wanted to make contacts with those allies against fascism when the conflict came." In 1939, just before World War II broke out in Europe, Prince Olav and Princess Martha visited the US. They soon became friends with Franklin and Eleanor Roosevelt. As crown prince, Olav received extensive military training. While his wife and 3 children lived in the US, Prince Olav worked from England with the underground and resistance movements against the Nazis, who had invaded and occupied Norway in 1940.

He provided much needed intelligence to President Roosevelt before the United States' entry into WW II. Prince Olav was respected by other allied leaders for his knowledge and leadership skills. He earned numerous war decorations from several countries, including the U.S. Legion of Merit.Olav became King Olav V of Norway in 1957 on the death of his father, King Haakon VII. He died in Norway in 1991.

Queen Zita 1892 - 1989

Princess Zita of Bourbon-Parma was the wife of Emperor Charles I of Austria. She was the last Empress consort of Austria and Queen consort of Bohemia and Hungary. After the end of World War I in 1918, the Emperor was deposed. Charles and Zita left in exile. Charles died at Madiera in 1922, when Zita was 28. She traveled from country to country with her 8 children. With the Nazi invasion of Belgium on May 10, 1940, Zita and her family became war refugees. Zita and her oldest son Otto became the symbols of unity for the exiled royal dynasty.

As exiles, the Habsburg family took the lead in resisting the Nazis in Austria. This foundered because of political opposition. Zita and her family came to the US in July of 1940. She visited Hyde Park. ER wrote, "The people of Europe were deeply troubled … and were looking for friends in other parts of the world — hence their sudden interest in the US."All her sons were active in the war effort. Otto promoted the dynasty's role in a post-war Europe and met regularly with Franklin Roosevelt. He, like other royals, provided much needed intelligence to FDR before the United States' entry into WW II. After the end of war in 1945, she spent the next two years touring the United States and Canada to raise funds for war-ravaged Austria and Hungary. Queen Zita died in Austria in 1989.

Queen Wilhelmina 1880—1962

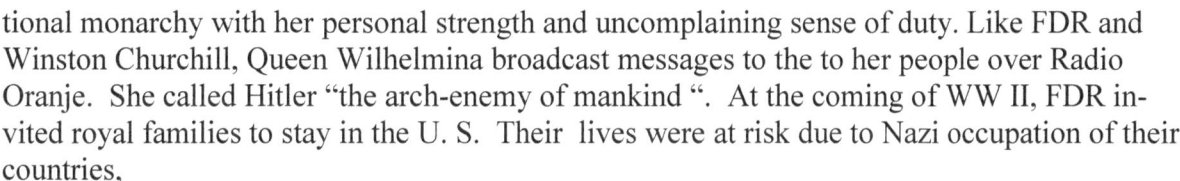

In May of 1940, the Germans invaded Holland. 2 days later the entire Dutch royal family was evacuated to England by ship, sent by King George VI of Great Britain.

Queen Wilhelmina established her government-in-exile in London. She was widowed in 1934. She carried on the duties of her constitutional monarchy with her personal strength and uncomplaining sense of duty. Like FDR and Winston Churchill, Queen Wilhelmina broadcast messages to the to her people over Radio Oranje. She called Hitler "the arch-enemy of mankind ". At the coming of WW II, FDR invited royal families to stay in the U. S. Their lives were at risk due to Nazi occupation of their countries,

ER wrote "He wanted to make contacts with those allies against fascism when the conflict came."In the summer of 1942, Queen Wilhelmina and her daughter, Princess Juliana, along with Juliana's children, visited the Roosevelts. In England, she developed ideas about a new political and social life for the Dutch after the liberation. When the Netherlands was liberated in 1945, the Queen was disappointed to see the same political factions taking power as before the war. Queen Wilhelmina died in the Netherlands in 1962.

Princess Juliana 1901-2004

In 1937, Princess Juliana married Prince Bernhard of Germany. The couple had 4 daughters: Princess Beatrix, Princess Irene, Princess Margriet, and Princess Christina. In May of 1940, the Germans invaded Holland. 2 days later the entire Dutch royal family was evacuated to England by ship, sent by King George VI of Great Britain.

Princess Juliana, only child of Queen Wilhelmina of the Netherlands, took her daughters to Canada for their safety. Their third daughter was born in Ottawa in 1943 and named Margriet. FDR was one of her godparents.

At the coming of WW II FDR invited royal families to stay in the U. S. Their lives were at risk due to Nazi occupation of their countries. ER wrote ,"He wanted to make contacts with those allies against fascism when the conflict came." In the summer of 1942, Queen Wilhelmina and her daughter, Princess Juliana, along with Juliana's children, visited the Roosevelts. While her mother visited Hyde Park only once, Juliana and her children visited often. Juliana had a summer home in western Massachusetts, and the trip to Hyde Park was an easy drive.

After WW II, Princess Juliana returned to Holland and worked tirelessly to provide aid to the war-torn country. Princess Juliana died, as Queen Juliana, in the Netherlands in 2004.

Sara Delano Roosevelt 1855 - 1941

Sara Delano was the wife and widow of James Roosevelt, and the mother of Franklin Delano Roosevelt, the 32nd President of the United States. Mrs. Roosevelt became the owner of Springwood when her husband, James, died in 1900. She retained ownership and successful management of the estate until her death. As the mother of the president, she was the hostess of Springwood during the many visits of world dignitaries and heads of state who were invited by her son Franklin and daughter-in-law Eleanor.

Springwood became an extension of the White House for use in presidential diplomacy. FDR is one of the first presidents to use his private home in this manner. Always the attentive mother, Sara Roosevelt took the time to write to her son Franklin as he became governor of New York state (at age 46) to remind him to write his signature with care and dignity on official documents and correspondence! Mrs. Roosevelt died at Springwood in 1941 at age 86.

Franklin D. Roosevelt 1882 - 1945

Franklin Roosevelt, son of James and Sara Roosevelt was born at Springwood on January 30, 1882. Due to his mother's medical complications during birth, FDR was James and Sara's only child. When he married Eleanor Roosevelt in 1905, he made Springwood their home. Their children were raised here.

FDR loved Springwood more than any other place in his life. Wherever he was in the world, he always made time to come home, as if this place was his touchstone in life.

During his life, he held many important positions leading up to his presidency … state senator for New York, vice-presidential candidate, assistant secretary of the Navy, governor of New York state, and then president. FDR became ill with the crippling viral disease polio in 1921 at the age of 39, leaving his legs paralyzed. *He is the first profoundly disabled president to be elected.*
He is the only 4 term president in our history. During the last year of his life, FDR wrote, "Everything within me cries out to go back to my home on the Hudson River."

FDR died on April 12, 1945, at Warm Springs, Georgia

Eleanor Roosevelt 1884 - 1962

Anna Eleanor Roosevelt, daughter of Anna Hall and Elliott Roosevelt, was the niece of President Theodore Roosevelt. Both of her parents died by the time she was 10 years old. Her childhood was troubled by family strictness, ridicule, and her own timid personality. Eleanor conquered her fears as she became comfortable with a formal education in England, and enjoyed travels through Europe for the first time.

She met her distant cousin Franklin socially; they fell in love and married in 1905. They were 20 and 22 years old when they married. Eleanor and Franklin had 6 children together. 5 of whom reached adulthood ... Anna, James, Elliott, Franklin Jr., and John. Their first Franklin Jr., died in infancy. ER never felt that Springwood was her home - it was her mother-in-law's domain.

She became more confident in her life as a wife and mother as well as in her career of public service. Her life's work was as a world humanitarian. She served at the United Nations, and for other causes such as civil rights until her death in 1962 in New York.

Anna Roosevelt 1906 - 1975

As the only daughter and eldest child in the family, Anna, or "Sis", as she was called, enjoyed an especially close relationship with her father. Anna was closer to her father than her mother. She worked as her father's assistant for a brief time during the war. Her relationship with ER improved as Anna matured. During the last seventeen years of ER's life, they were very close and wrote each other often.

She choose not to pursue a college education after briefly attending Cornell University. FDR's children resented that they each had to have an appointment to see the president. Anna's 3 marriages produced 3 children: Anna Eleanor ("Sistie"), Curtis ("Buzzie"), and John Roosevelt Boettiger. At FDR's insistence, she moved into the White House in 1944 while her husband John Boettiger was overseas. She remained at the White House until FDR's death in 1945, one of the companions and confidantes who surrounded the president in the last year of his life.

After ER's death in 1962, Anna was active with organizations and causes that her mother had supported. This includes Americans for Democratic Action, the United Nations Association of the United States and the Wiltwyck School. Anna also served as a board member of the Eleanor Roosevelt Memorial Foundation. She died in New York in 1975.

Franklin D. Roosevelt, Jr. 1914– 1988

Franklin Delano Roosevelt, Jr., is the fifth child of Franklin and
Eleanor Roosevelt. Known in the family as "Brother" or "Brud,"
he and the Roosevelts' youngest son, John, spent considerable time
with ER during their childhoods, in part because of FDR's paralysis. At the same time, his interest in politics enabled Franklin Jr. to
forge a close relationship with his father.

After graduating from Groton and Harvard, Franklin Jr. studied
law at the University of Virginia. He was admitted to the bar in 1942. FDR's children resented
that they each had to have an appointment to see the president. Franklin Jr.'s 5 marriages produced 5 children: Franklin D III, Christopher D., Nancy S., Laura D., and John A Roosevelt.

He was called to active duty from the Naval Reserve in 1941 as an ensign in the U. S. Navy.
He was awarded the Purple Heart Medal and the Silver Star; FDR Jr.'s own political career was
the most active of the Roosevelt children.   He served 3 terms in Congress representing New
York. He was appointed to cabinet and staff positions by Presidents Kennedy and Johnson.
After 1966, Franklin Jr. became increasingly involved in business, farming in NY state, and
Roosevelt-related organizations. He died in New York in 1988.

John A. Roosevelt 1916 - 1981

John Aspinwall Roosevelt, (called Johnnie) the sixth and last child of
Eleanor and Franklin Roosevelt, was a businessman, philanthropist. John
and his brother, Franklin, Jr., were much closer to ER than the 3 older
Roosevelt children had been. In part because by the time they were born,
ER was more comfortable as a parent, and in part because she acted for
FDR in their upbringing due to the polio that disabled FDR when John
was five years old.

He was married twice. His first marriage produced 4 children: Haven, Anne S., Sara D., an
Joan L. Educated at Groton and Harvard, in 1941 John then volunteered for duty with the U.
S. Navy to serve in World War II. He was discharged in 1946 as lieutenant commander.
FDR's children resented that they each had to have an appointment to see the president. John
was the only Republican in the family. He was also the only Roosevelt son who did not have
political ambitions. John and his family moved into Stone Cottage next door to ER's home at
Val-Kill in 1950. This enabled ER to live safely at Val-Kill until the year of her death in 1962.
In retirement by 1980, his philanthropic activities centered on Roosevelt-related organizations
and included fundraising for the National Foundation for Infantile Paralysis, which FDR had
founded. He died in New York in 1981.

James Roosevelt 1828 - 1900

James Roosevelt, Franklin's father was a strong and abiding influence in Franklin's life, even though he died of heart disease in 1900 when Franklin was only 18 years old. As the only child of James and Sara Roosevelt, Franklin was precious to both of them. His father would take special interest in his upbringing and education, as well as his protection. When Franklin was quite young, James paid the farm children a bounty for capturing and killing poisonous snakes found in Franklin's play area.

James loved to take Franklin on horseback with him to tour the estate. He taught Franklin about the farm operation, love of the land, birds and nature, and the river. It was because of his father's influence that FDR became interested in conservation law when he began his political life.

Written descriptions say he was stern, forthright, but fair in his dealings with people. His was an early, but life-lasting influence on Franklin. Sara Roosevelt's goal was that her son would be just like his father … "straight and honorable, just and kind." James Roosevelt died in NY in 1900.

Anna Roosevelt 1906 - 1975

As the only daughter and eldest child in the family, Anna, or "Sis", as she was called, enjoyed an especially close relationship with her father. Anna was closer to her father than her mother. She worked as her father's assistant for a brief time during the war.

Her relationship with ER improved as Anna matured. During the last seventeen years of ER's life, they were very close and wrote each other often. She choose not to pursue a college education after briefly attending Cornell University.

FDR's children resented that they each had to have an appointment to see the president. Anna's 3 marriages produced 3 children: Anna Eleanor ("Sistie"), Curtis ("Buzzie"), and John Roosevelt Boettiger. At FDR's insistence, she moved into the White House in 1944 while her husband John Boettiger was overseas. She remained at the White House until FDR's death in 1945, one of the companions and confidantes who surrounded the president in the last year of his life.

After ER's death in 1962, Anna was active with organizations and causes that her mother had supported. This includes Americans for Democratic Action, the United Nations Association of the United States and the Wiltwyck School. Anna also served as a board member of the Eleanor Roosevelt Memorial Foundation. She died in New York in 1975.

James Roosevelt 1907 - 1991

James Roosevelt, ("Jimmy") the second child and first son of Franklin and Eleanor Roosevelt, was, apart from his sister, Anna, the Roosevelt child most active in FDR's political career. He worked on FDR's 1932 presidential campaign and served officially and unofficially as his father's assistant. After graduating from Groton and Harvard, a family tradition, James was a partner in a Boston insurance company. In 1937, he joined his father's staff as presidential assistant.

FDR's children resented that they each had to have an appointment to see the president. After the attack on Pearl Harbor in 1941, he chose combat duty and was awarded both the Navy Cross and the Silver Star. His 4 marriages produced 6 children: Sara D., Kate, James, Jr., Michael, Anna Eleanor, Hall D., and Rebecca M. Roosevelt. Released from active duty in August 1945; he rank was brigadier general United States Marine Corps Reserve, retired. He worked for the Democratic Party from 1945 -1955. From 1955 until 1967, he served as a congressman for California.

In later years, James worked for the improvement of the Social Security system as well. He was a resident of Newport Beach, California, until his death there in 1991.

Elliott Roosevelt 1910 - 1990

Elliott Roosevelt, ("Bunny" as he was called by FDR) second surviving son of the Roosevelts, ultimately became the most controversial of the Roosevelt children. He was named after ER's father and was ER's favorite child. However, ER's favoritism led to tensions among the other Roosevelt children. His 5 marriages produced 9 children: William D., Ruth C., Elliott, Jr., David B., including adoption of Patricia Whitehead's five children.

Elliott Roosevelt was a bombardier in the United States Army Air Forces (USAAF) during World War II. As an Army pilot, he and his crew played a key role in the D-Day landings in 1944. As a military aide, he accompanied FDR to the Casablanca, Cairo, and Tehran Conferences. Elliott attained the rank of Brigadier General in 1945. He was an author of several books both fictional mysteries, and non-fiction about his parents and family. Elliott was involved in many different careers during his life; including a Texas radio station owner, a rancher, and for a term in the 1960s as the mayor of Miami Beach, Florida. Elliott Roosevelt died in 1990 at the age of 80 in Arizona.

Endicott Peabody

At the age of fourteen Franklin attended the Groton School in Massachusetts, where
Endicott Peabody was the head master. Franklin looked up to the Reverend Peabody, learning many lessons from him.

"It used to bother me when I made mistakes and wasted a lot of
time fretting. Now I have learned that if one does the best he can in the light of all his available knowledge and
judgment, then… there is no use grieving over it. I do the best I can under the circumstances and go on to something else. One thing at a time is a great thing"

Mademoiselle Sandoz

Franklin's Education as a young person took place at home. He was tutored by
Mademoiselle Sandoz who was a French
speaking Swedish woman. She had high
expectations of Franklin and once said to him "Your father is wasting his money and I am wasting my time, and I shall leave you."

Looking back from the White House, in 1933 Franklin Roosevelt wrote his old teacher , Mademoiselle Sandoz, "I have often thought
it was you, more than anyone else who laid a foundation of my education. The lessons in French which I began at that time have stood me in good stead all these years, and here in Washington it is great pleasure to be able to converse with members of the Diplomatic Corps in a common tongue."